Poems of Love:

A Selection

Volume 1

Gary W. Burns

Turning Corner Books ™

WWW.TURNINGCORNERBOOKS.COM

Library of Congress Control Number: 2010927202
ISBN: 978-0-9845342-8-9

Fifth Printing, October 2025

Manufactured in the United States
Designed by the author; artwork and photos by the author.

Photos -
Jacket: Orchids, Brooklyn Botanical Gardens, Brooklyn, NY
Page 15: Travelers, Self Portrait
Page 39: Orchids, Brooklyn Botanical Garden, Brooklyn, NY
Page 59: The Open Sea
Page 77: Bali Seashore

This ISBN was previously printed under the title *Warm:
Reflections* (out of print). Some of the original poems were
rewritten and some titles were changed. Also, some poems from
the First and Second Printings were removed and replaced by
poems from the following books by Gary W. Burns:

Bridges: To There (Poems for the Mind, Body & Spirit)
Clouds: On the Wind (Poems for the Soul - A Meditation)
Moments: This To The Next

Other Books of Poetry by Gary W. Burns

Bridges: To There
  (Poems for Mind, Body & Spirit)

Clouds: On the Wind
  (Poems for the Soul – A Meditation)

Earth Tones: A Journey
  (Poetry for the Journey)

Garden Walks: Hand In Hand
  (Poems To Relax By)

Moments: This to the Next
  (Poetry - Now and Eternity)

Rainy Day: Wondering
  (Poems for a Rainy Day)

To You With Love: Selected Poems

Twilight: Awaking the Stars
  (Poems of the Night's Light)

To Sylvia
for her gift of insight

❀ ❀ ❀ ❀ ❀ ❀ ❀ ❀ ❀ ❀

Contents

Travelers

Welcome	17
Travelers	18
Love and You	20
Natures Care	21
Worth the Wait	22
Wonder	23
Come to Know	24
For You	25
Who Knows	26
Strolling With You	28
Sway	29
Sets Aglow	30
Beauty *In Poems of Love*	31
The Spirit of Love	32
Release	33
Waimea Bay	34
Life the River	36
Collecting Things	37

One Another

Today 41

The Willow 42

The Pair 43

Choices 44

The Passage To 45

Seeing One Another 46

And Know Them 47

Lazy Clouds 48

Each Day 49

The Embrace 50

Softly 51

Love Tells Me 52

Of Reflection 53

Awake 54

By And By 55

Of Love 56

Maybe Love's 57

Being Love

Being Love   61

Journey   62

Be Peacefully   64

One Love   66

Cipher   67

Memories   68

Quietude   69

Mystery   70

Accomplish   71

Fate   72

By Any Name   73

Warm Reflections   74

Cosmos   75

Sky-Sea Harmony

Seafaring   79

Along the Waterfront   80

The Loving Heart   82

All In All   83

By Chance   84

Voyaging   85

Nothing More Dear   86

Eternity Lovingly   88

Intimate   89

To Somewhere Out There   90

Nurturing   92

Loving Eyes
    In Poems of Love   93

You Are   94

Solution   95

Dearest Friend   96

The Way   97

Love Knows   98

Travelers

Welcome

Welcome
To this peaceful place

Where sounds
Are soft.

Here the edge
Of every word

Is smooth
And sooths

The solitary
Soul.

Travelers

1

The waiting buds
Are set
And ready
For spring;
I'm ready too,
Ready
For you.

2

Come with me,
Please.

There's a journey
Warm
And
Kind
That's yours
And mine.

3

Through days
Then years
Through smiles
And tears
We'll travel.

4

We'll warm
Beside loves flame
And in the flicker
Discover
Each the other
To be a lover.

Love and You

*Where you're going
I'm going there too.*

I'm with you.

Natures Care

Beauty

Moving
Tree to tree
And within
The green scenery
Reaches
You and me

Offering
The pleasantness

Of peace,
Bliss
And happiness.

Go with open arms
To there,
Share
Natures care.

Worth the Wait

1

A love may come
And stay, or
Simply come
Then go away.

Our needs and wants
Make no difference
For Love has
A mind of its own.

2

Here or gone,
Love's worth the wait
And the venture
We take.

Wonder

*Dynamic
Silence;*

Love

Come to Know

1

Be gentle
In the motion
Of you step.

With warmth
And kindness

Embrace
Each and every
Aspect of you.

2

Love
Within will grow
As you

You come
To know.

For You

*Happiness is
For you to be.*

Who Knows

1

The hills of Tuscany,
The autumn colors;
You.

2

What is it about love
That brings people together?

Perhaps, it's the love
In a loving touch
Or
The being held in reassuring arms.

I've heard it said
It's magic,
Some say it's grace.

3

Certainly,
It's beautiful;
A beauty not beyond, but
Now

Always now.

4

I love you.

Strolling
With You

Strolling the seashore
At the edge
Of life,

Together
We make our way
Along the day.

Sway

In the beauty
Of a child's face,
In that sacred
Space -

There,
Be captured
For a time
And let
The rhythm
And rhyme

Of love

Sway you
Lovingly.

Sets Aglow

How does one measure
The strength
Of a gentle touch.

I believe it's,
By the warmth
The heart
Comes to know

And the wonder
It sets aglow.

Beauty

Beauty;

The look
Of kind eyes
As their untold
Depths
Wed
The vastness of me.

In Poems Of Love

The Spirit
Of Love

Dear One,

Love
And I will care
*   for you.*

Yours always,
Love

Release

Where shadows
Lay long

And earth
Is cold

Ice last.

Release.

Kind heart,
Gentle touch;
Happiness.

Waimea Bay

1

Sitting on the shore at sunset;
Entertaining thoughts of the day.

2

All day long
People have come and gone;
Sun worshipers, surfboard kings,
A procession of sightseers.

Some leaving lingering images.
Others,
Once gone from view
Faded from thought.

3

Perhaps that's what's meant
By passing through or
Coming in and out of our lives.

4

Some people pass
Quickly through,
Gone
Once out of view.

Others, come and stay
A lifetime
Or perhaps a day
Or two.

5

So goes the way
As the sun sets
Here at Waimea Bay.

Life
The River

If you are going to go,
And because
Restless rivers
Never cease to flow,

I feel certain
You will;

Then go in love
My friend.

Collecting Things

I've collected things
From mountain streams,
Lakes, seas

And from beneath
Giant Sequoia trees.

And from many forest
I've lots
Of colorful leaves.

I put many a thing
In old mason jars:
O how one clings
To the small things.

But some things
You have to let go by;

There goes life,
By
With a loving smile
And an occasional sigh.

One Another

Today

Pour
In-to-me-you
Today,
In your loving way.

In Poems of Love

The Willow

The past won't last
And its twin the future
Is out sailing
On the sea Eternity;

So much for history,
So much for destiny.

Come
Be with me
Peacefully,
Beneath this willow tree
With wind dancing sway
Wooing.

The Pair

The cardinals:

He,
Red
Against
Leaf green;

She,
Gray-brown
Amongst
Shade and limb.

Him
  forever
  bringing:
Her
  forever
  bearing.

The pair. . .

Choices

A yes
Or a no
Can change
Your life,

Maybes
Don't count.

Let's love
One another.

The Passage To

I hope for you
A quiet moment
Opens up

And you move through
The passage to

Peacefulness;

It awaits you
To move through

Seeing
One Another

From
First moment thoughts
We made
Last minute
Decisions

And Know Them

May bliss
Be
Your life long companion

May happiness
Be
Your closest friend

Love

And know them

Lazy Clouds

The lazy clouds
Reflecting
In the sidewalk puddle
Remind me of me
With nothing to do.

They, lazily,
Drifting through
Wide sky blue
And me
Drifting along too.

Go ahead
Drift,
Make a lazy day for you

Too.

Each Day

We don't notice so much
The sun
Passing through the day,
But,
When sunset comes
We're amazed
At how quickly
It slips away.

Each day's
Worth giving in;
All of life's
Worth living in.

The Embrace

Warmth flowing,
Soul whirling,
Eyes wondrous

Embracing

Love

Softly

Dawn
Comes softly
To the day;

I want to love you
That way.

Love
Tells Me

Love
Tells me

Closeness
Is ecstasy

Let's be

Of Reflection

Capturing;

Sweet hellos

The warmth of hands

The smell of autumn

The sounds of spring

The sight
Of you, and you, and you

The taste of wine

And the feel
Of soft lips too

And saving them
For remembering when

Awake

Let's toss yesterday
To the wind
And give to tomorrow
A wish
That we may awake
Together,
In the peace
Of harmony.

By And By

Before going
Is gone

Love

Of Love

Infinitesimal;
Infinite . . .

Maybe Love's

Maybe love's

Gazing eyes
When they're filled
With the wonder
Of a sunset or sunrise

Maybe love's

More like, a touch
When it's in kindness
And the feel it brings
Is the song Love sings

Then again

Maybe love's
Your smile

Being Love

Being Love

Clouds,
Being clouds,
Go
Where the sun
Takes them.

Seas,
Being seas,
Go
Where the moon
Moves them.

You and I,
Being love,
Go
Where the heart
Leads us.

Journey

1

While
Crossing
The bridge
Journey -

2

Traveling
The road
Life

3

Walking
The sidewalk
Hope

4

Searching
Through the rain
Time

5

I find
My-
Self

In the arms
Of Love

6

Please
Join me

Be Peacefully

1

So many people needing
To be with people

And me
Wanting
To be alone

2

So many find less
In being alone

3

Me,
I find
So much more

4

A place where
Thoughts gather
Harmoniously
And I peacefully be

5

Here's wishing
You "Be"

Peacefully

One Love

Morning was asked,
"Morning
Do you miss
    the night?"

Morning's light
Replied,
"I'm holding
    her hand
      isn't Love
        grand."

Cipher

No matter
what the
challenge
the password is
Love.

Memories

Leaving the candle
Lit
Through the night

For the sake
Of shadows
And dancing light:

Memories.

Quietude

Quietude,

Can set you free

Lovingly

Mystery

Love
Leaves me
In mystery

A mystery
To let Be

Accomplish

You won't know
If you don't

And

You have to
To do:

Come on.

Fate

Trying to make sense
Of it all

But
Deciding

There's no sense
To be made

And counting it fate:

Walking through
Dreams with you.

By Any Name

1

*The rhythm
Of the universe*

*The beating
Of the heart*

*One in the same
By any name*

2

Love

Warm Reflections

Gentleness
Comes lovingly

In warm
Reflections

Cosmos

From sunlit morning
To and through
Moon bright night

Each day
Lives this way:

O this symphony of hearts.

Sky-Sea Harmony

Seafaring

Love;

Sailing its sea

Keeps me.

Set sail.

Along
The Waterfront

1

Evening's
Red-skied-sleepiness
Drifts
Below
The rim of the world.

Stars,
Twinkling on ebony,
Slowly
Grace the night.

2

Unwound
And love ready
We start our voyage
Of discovery.

3

Voyaging
We make our way
Along the waterfront.

Coasting up
Then coasting down,
Charting
Landmarks by touch
And waypoints
By sound.

4

Searching for harbors:
Safe places from the storms.

Full Orchestra - Strings

The Loving Heart

The place

That knows not
The sands of time

Nor a space
Called empty, full
Or in between

That place

The Loving Heart

All In All

For these brief moments
Of time
You give me heartbeats
Of love

For all else
        Love boundless

By Chance

Those times
Come rare

While
They are there

Take them

Voyaging

Bound by the calling
Of the open sea

Wayfarer

Come close to me;
Let's sail Love
Toward Destiny.

Nothing More Dear

1

Like some great falls,
The melting snow
Rushes
From the roof top.

Racing
It goes
Past the window
And diverts
Into a multitude
Of sliver sunlit streams.

2

To me
There is nothing
More dear
Then you
Laying the day long
Here
Beside me

Watching
Silver sunlit streams.

Eternity Lovingly

Filling you
Filling me

Eternity's
Touch

Love
Is that much

Intimate

Silently
I come to you
And silently
You come to me

Ever so
We are joined

Eternally

To Somewhere Out There

1

The birds,
On their way to somewhere,
Visited the backyard today.

The small flock quickly
Landed.

Foraged.

Then quickly
Went away.

2

I had no idea
Where they were going.
And perhaps,
Neither did they.

I guess, in a way,
We're like the birds;
We can't get from here
To that somewhere
Unless we go.

And so,
We make our way
Day by day
To somewhere
Out there.

Nurturing

Yesterday
They spoke of you
And today
They do too

Rain drops

Nurturing:

Love

Loving Eyes

We say so many things
Without a word spoken

In Poems Of Love

You Are

You are

Beautiful.

Solution

Love all things;

The heart
In harmony

Sings.

Dearest Friend

Dress your heart
In this,
Beauties attire

And be love

Yours warmly,
Bliss

The Way

Be
Not the moment,
Nor the hour,
Nor the day;
But,
The way -
Love.

Love

knows no

dichotomy

About the Author

Inspired by nature and the beauty around him Gary W. Burns started writing poetry at a young age. Early on Gary was able to express his thoughts, ideas and emotions through the vivid imagery of his verse. His poetry has been published in various literary arts journals, anthologies and magazines. He is the author of 10 books of poetry. Through his poems Gary shares his reflections on the many facets of life and on the beauty of nature. The expressiveness of his poetry has been enriched by his wide reading in philosophy and psychology. He has traveled throughout the world and has lived in numerous countries, to include, Italy, Korea, Saudi Arabia and Canada. He has also lived in Hawaii and several other states. Currently, Gary makes his home in Northern Virginia near the foothills of the Blue Ridge Mountains.

ENJOY THESE OTHER BOOKS OF POETRY BY GARY W. BURNS

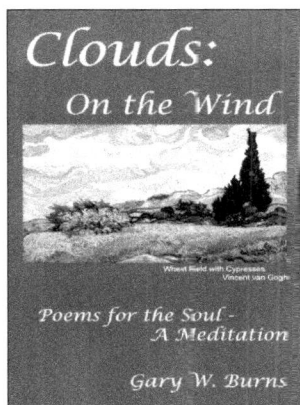

Clouds: On the Wind
(Poems for the Soul - A Meditation)
ISBN: 978-0-9845342-0-2 (Paperback)
ISBN: 978-0-9845342-1-0 (Hardcover)
ISBN: 978-0-9860900-3-5 (E-Book)

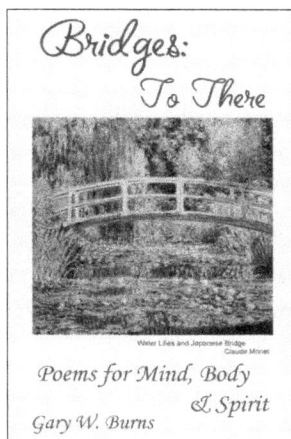

Bridges: To There
(Poems for the Mind, Body & Spirit)
ISBN: 978-0-9827805-6-5 (Paperback)
ISBN: 978-0-9827805-7-2 (Hardcover)
ISBN: 978-0-9860900-3-5 (E-Book)

Earth Tones: A Journey
(Poetry for the Journey)
ISBN: 978-0-9845342-6-5 (Paperback)
ISBN: 978-0-9845342-9-6 (Hardcover)
ISBN: 978-0-9860900-8-0 (E-Book)

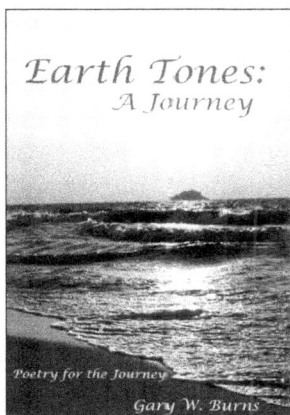

Available at WWW.TURNINGCORNERBOOKS.COM and where books are sold.

Dawn and Beyond: Embark
(Poetry – Come Destiny)
ISBN: 978-0-9827805-8-9 (Paperback)
ISBN: 978-0-9827805-9-6 (Hardcover)
ISBN: 978-0-9860900-0-4 (E-Book)

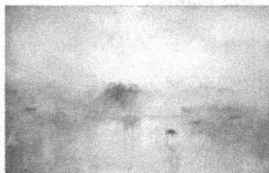

Garden Walks: Hand In Hand
(Poems To Relax By)
ISBN: 978-0-9845342-3-4
(Paperback)
ISBN: 978-0-9827805-0-3 (Hardcover)
ISBN: 978-0-9860900-1-1 (E-Book)

Rainy Day: Wondering
(Poems for a Rainy Day)
ISBN: 978-0-9845342-5-8 (Paperback)
ISBN: 978-0-9827805-2-7 (Hardcover)
ISBN: 978-0-9860900-7-3 (E-Book)

Available at WWW.TURNINGCORNERBOOKS.COM and where books are sold.

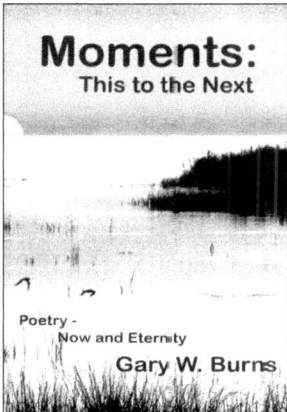

www.ingramcontent.com/pod-product-compliance
Lightning Source LLC
Chambersburg PA
CBHW072151020426
42334CB00018B/1954